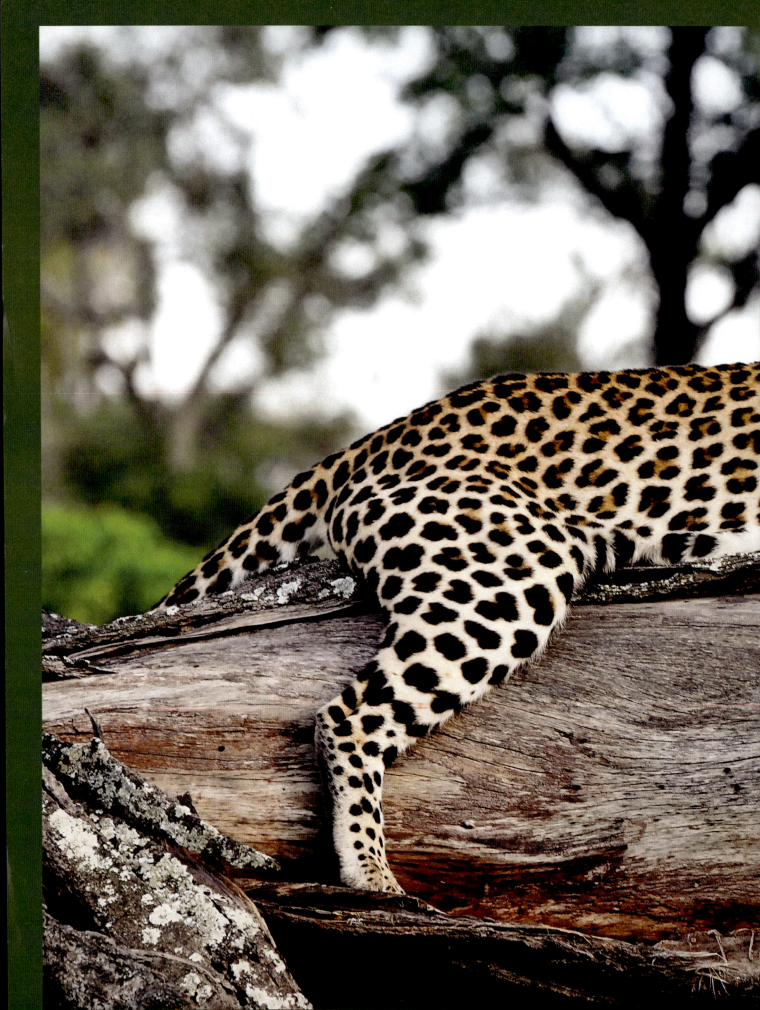

Leopard

BY TYLER GRADY

Dylanna Press

Leopards are **mammals** that can be found in Africa, Asia, India, and China. Their range is the most widespread of all big cats.

There are nine subspecies of leopards including the Sri Lankan, Amur, Arabian, Javan, Indian, North Chinese, Persian, Indochinese, and African leopards.

They are related to lions, tigers, cheetahs, jaguars, and other types of cats. Their scientific name is *Panthera pardus* and they belong to the Felidae family.

---

mammals – warm-blooded animals with hair or fur that give birth to live young

One of the most recognizable members of the animal kingdom, leopards are known for their incredible strength and distinctive spotted coats.

Leopards are the smallest members of the large cat family. They weigh between 45 to 165 pounds (20 to 75 kg) and average 3 to 6 feet (.9 to 1.8 m) in length with an additional 2 to 3 foot (.6 to .9 meter) tail. Males are much larger than females.

Leopards have long muscular bodies with shorter legs, large heads, and rounded ears. They have light yellow to darker orange colored fur covered with dark **rosettes**. Some leopards can be all black, these are often called black panthers.

---

rosettes – irregular-shaped spots

Leopards live in many **habitats** including deserts, grasslands, mountains and rainforests. They tend to prefer areas with trees that can provide them cover.

They are extremely adaptable animals and can live in both cold and warm climates.

Unfortunately, at least 75 percent of their historical range has been lost to human activities such as agriculture and settlement.

---

habitat – surroundings or conditions in which an animal lives

The leopard has many physical **adaptations** to its environment.

Their fur acts as **camouflage,** helping them to blend in with their surroundings and go undetected by both their prey and predators.

Leopards have well-developed senses of hearing, smell, and vision. They can see very well at night, making them excellent nighttime hunters.

They have curved claws, which allow them to climb trees and keep a strong grip on their prey. In addition, their muscular legs let them run very fast and jump high into the air. These adaptations make them very efficient predators.

---

adaptations – ways in which a species becomes fitted into its natural environment to increase its chance of survival

camouflage – a mechanism used to disguise appearance

Leopards are **carnivores**. Their preferred food source is medium-sized **herbivores** such as gazelles and antelope. However, they are flexible eaters and will consume just about any animal that is available including monkeys, birds, fish, cheetah cubs, rodents, and dung beetles.

Leopards typically do not eat every day. They will consume between 6 to 8 pounds (2.7 to 3.6 kg) at once and then go for several days before hunting again.

If they capture a large animal, they will save it and eat the **carrion** over the course of up to two weeks.

---

carnivore – animal that only eats meat

herbivore – animal that eats plants

carrion – dead and decaying animal

Leopards are **solitary** hunters who typically hunt at night.

They prefer to stalk and **ambush** their prey by waiting in hiding and slowly creeping up on their target. When the animal is within striking distance they will make a brief charge and pounce. Once the animal is down, the leopard will bite its throat or back of the neck.

Leopards do not chase their prey over long distances. If their initial attack is unsuccessful they will give up and wait for another chance.

Leopards do not need to drink water. Instead they get their **hydration** from the animals they eat.

---

solitary – done or existing alone

ambush – surpise attack from a concealed position

hydration – the aborption of water

Leopards are **polygamous**, with both males and females mating with more than one partner. Mating can take place at any time of year. Leopards reach maturity between two and four years old.

After conception takes place, the male leopard leaves and has nothing to do with the female or her future cubs.

Pregnancy lasts an average of 100 days and female leopards typically give birth to between two to three cubs at a time.

---

polygamous – having more than one mate at a time

Baby leopards are born blind and helpless. The mother leopard takes care of them by herself, keeping them safe and providing food. They do not leave their den until they are about three months old.

Leopard mothers are very protective and will stay with their cubs almost all of the time, leaving only to hunt. They will move the cubs from den to den in order to avoid predators.

For the first three months of their life they survive only on their mother's milk. After this they start eating meat and by 8 months start learning to hunt.

Once they reach 18 to 24 months, the cubs are ready to go out into the world on their own.

Leopards love to sleep! They average about 18 hours per day. This is needed to preserve and recharge their energy levels.

They are generally **nocturnal** animals who sleep during the day and are most active at night, prowling in search of food.

Leopards are excellent climbers and a lot of their sleeping takes places hidden in the branches of trees or tucked away in caves.

---

nocturnal – active at night, asleep during the day

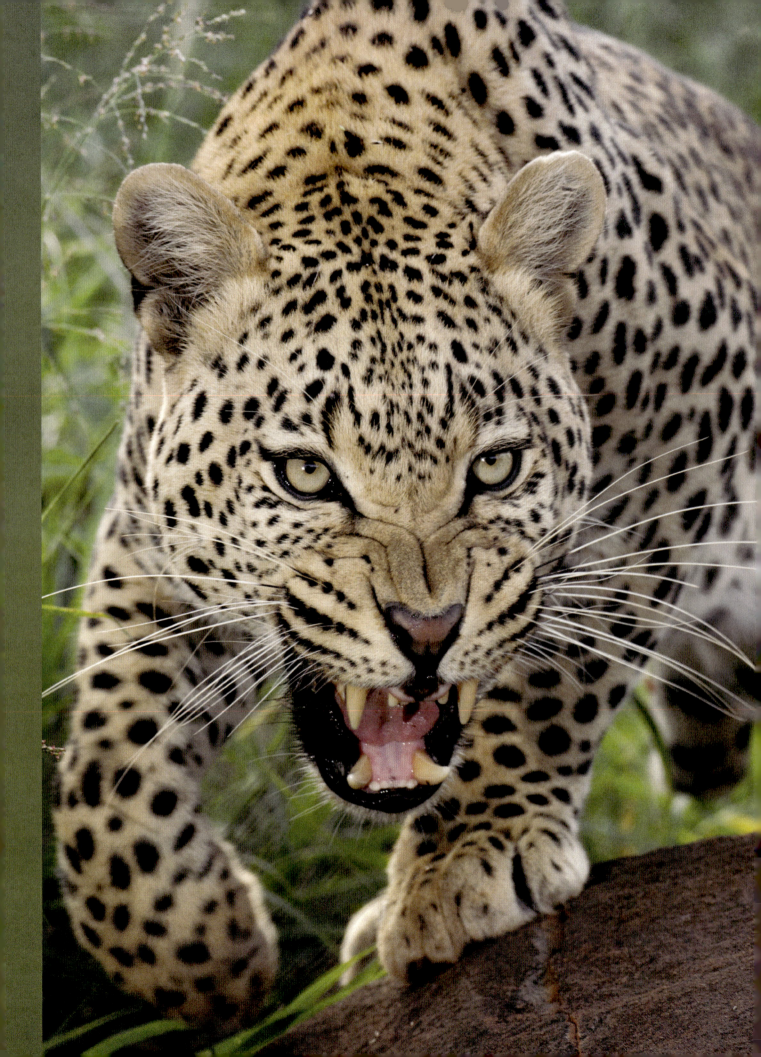

Leopards are **solitary** animals who spend the majority of their lives alone, with the exception of a mother leopard and her cubs. Adult leopards only interact during mating.

When they do communicate they use distinctive **vocalizations** such as coughs, chuffs, growls, and even purrs.

Leopards are **territorial** and will roam across and defend a range large enough to provide them with an adequate supply of food. A male leopard's range is larger than a female's and can overlap with several female leopards.

To mark their territory, leopards will leave scent marks and scratches on trees.

_____

solitary – done or existing alone

territorial – an animal that defends a specific area of land

vocalizations – the sounds an animal makes

The average lifespan of a leopard in the wild is 10 to 12 years. They can live twenty years or more in captivity.

It is very hard to estimate how many leopards there are in the wild but the population has been on the decline for many years.

They are listed as an **endangered species** in Asia and the Middle East. In Africa they are considered a **vulnerable species**.

---

endangered species – species considered to be facing a serious risk of extinction in the wild

vulnerable species – species considered to be facing a high risk of extinction in the wild

While predators themselves, leopards are also **prey** to animals such as lions, tigers, and packs of hyenas.

Humans are by far the biggest threats to leopards. Expanding human populations threaten leopards through habitat destruction and fragmentation.

Poaching also contributes to leopard deaths. Leopards are hunted for trophies and for their fur and teeth.

They are also killed when they come into conflict with human settlements such as preying on livestock.

---

prey – animal that is hunted and killed by another animal for food

poaching – illegal killing and trafficking of animals

Leopards are beautiful and elusive animals. They are symbols of strength, grace, and agility and are one of the world's most recognizable animals.

Unfortunately, leopards continued existence is in doubt due to loss of habitat, hunting, and conflicts with humans.

Conservation efforts are underway but it remains to be seen if this amazing big cat can survive in the coming decades.

---

conservation – protecting natural resources for future generations

Word Search

```
E O O C N D U G X G N I T N U H
R V I H G C A S O L I T A R Y I
O C V E Z J A M R L R M E R B P
V U W R T S R M H S U B M A K F
I K A B D D O V O O A C A E M R
N V X I Y Y T D Z U R B T H A O
R J Y V Q I A B L L F S K N M S
A P Y O R L D S W E E L O Y M E
C Y O R S Z E T M I O I A Q A T
R G Q E G W R N C D R P M G L T
X Y F C M W P E E R U J A K E E
S E N S E S P T A W T S F R Z S
F Y F J G S T C N X T U D Z D I
U E M W B O N O I T A T P A D A
D A I U P P Q I F V M C F O Q S
M D S S H H A B I T A T K H O X
```

ADAPTATION	CARRION	LEOPARD	SENSES
AMBUSH	HABITAT	MAMMAL	SOLITARY
CAMOUFLAGE	HERBIVORE	PREDATOR	SPOTTED
CARNIVORE	HUNTING	ROSETTES	SUBSPECIES

INDEX

adaptations, 11
ambush, 15
black panthers, 7
camouflage, 11
carnivores, 12
carrion, 12
characteristics, 7, 11
claws, 11
climate, 8
climbing, 20
communication, 23
conservation, 28
cubs, 16, 19, 23
diet, 12
endangered species, 24
Felidae family, 4
food sources, 12
fur, 7
habitat, 8
habitat destruction, 27, 28
hearing, 11
herbivores, 12
humans, 8, 27
hunting, 12, 15, 19, 27
hydration, 15
lifespan, 24
livestock, 27

mammals, 4
mating, 16
nocturnal, 20
Panthera pardus, 4
parenting, 19, 23
physical adaptations, 11
physical appearance, 7
poaching, 27
polygamous, 16
population, 24
pregnancy, 16
prey, 12, 27
range, 4, 8, 23
rosettes, 7
senses, 11
size, 7
sleep habits, 20
smell, 11
socialization, 23
subspecies, 4
territory, 4, 23
threats, 27, 28
trees, 11, 20
vision, 11
vocalization, 23
vulnerable species, 24
water, 15

Published by Dylanna Press an imprint of Dylanna Publishing, Inc.
Copyright © 2022 by Dylanna Press
Author: Tyler Grady
All rights reserved. No part of this publication may be reproduced, stored in a retrieval system, or transmitted by any means, including electronic, mechanical, photocopying, or otherwise, without prior written permission of the publisher.

Although the publisher has taken all reasonable care in the preparation of this book, we make no warranty about the accuracy or completeness of its content and, to the maximum extent permitted, disclaim all liability arising from its use.

Printed in the U.S.A.

Made in United States
Orlando, FL
18 May 2025

61378437R00019